Writing

Strands

A COMPLETE WRITING PROGRAM
USING A PROCESS APPROACH
TO WRITING AND COMPOSITION

ASSURING
CONTINUITY AND CONTROL

LEVEL 2

of
a complete writing program
for homeschoolers

a
publication
of

NATIONAL WRITING INSTITUTE
624 W. University #248
Denton, TX 76201-1889

Manufactured in the United States of America

ISBN 1-888344-12-1

For information: National Writing Institute,
                  624 W. University #248
                  Denton, TX 76201-1889

                  (800) 688-5375
                  info@writingstrands.com

Cover art by Matt Payovich

NATIONAL WRITING INSTITUTE PUBLICATIONS

STUDENTS

Writing Strands Level 1
Writing Strands Level 2
Writing Strands Level 3
Writing Strands Level 4
Writing Strands Level 5
Writing Strands Level 6
Writing Strands Level 7
Writing Exposition
Creating Fiction

Communication And Interpersonal Relationships

Dragonslaying Is For Dreamers
Axel Meets The Blue Men
Axel's Challenge

PARENTS/TEACHERS

Evaluating Writing

Reading Strands

Analyzing The Novel:
Dragonslaying Is For Dreamers

Essays on Writing

INTRODUCTION

This group of exercises in the series called *Writing Strands* is designed to give homeschooled second grade students a grounding in the very complicated process of giving others their thoughts in written form.

The teaching of this skill is one of the hardest jobs that you have. These exercises will make it easier. Much of the planning and detail of the writing process is presented here.

These exercises are written for you to teach from. This is the only book in the series in which the expectation is that the child cannot work alone. Most seven year olds are too inexperienced to work independently. But, rather than increase your work, this writing process should make it easier for both you and your child to meet the demands for student writing skill. I strongly recommend that you get our book *Evaluating Writing*. It will save you a great deal of time, and it will save your children much pain.

I have referred to your child in this book in the plural, because I really don't feel comfortable using a singular and then referring to that person as they or using their. It is very common now and sounds like this: Ask your child to write this sentence and then check their work. Wow, does that grate my teeth. I'm not a purist, but there are limits. I also can't use the very awkward he/she solution. Too cumbersome for me. On the first draft of this book I used he with the first exercise and used she with the second and alternated throughout. Awful! So, you'll just have to change the words in your mind when you're working with just one child.

Although *Writing Strands* was not written for grade-level working, this level two book has been designed for students who are at the second grade level. When a child independently can write the sentence The dog is big, that child is ready for this level.

The language arts program using the books in this series are designed for one school year, which should include our reading program. We recommend that you alternate weekly each writing exercise with reading and discussing books and ideas. In this way you will have a full school year of language arts. If you do this it will mean that one week you will not assign work in *Writing Strands* but concentrate on reading and discussing ideas with your child, and the next week you will work with an exercise from *Writing Strands*.

The reading half of any language arts program should involve reading and talking about books and ideas. National Writing Institute's *Reading Strands* is designed to do just that for you and your children.

CONTENTS

HOW TO MAKE *WRITING STRANDS* WORK FOR YOU

1. Your children should have writing folders containing all written work which should be kept for their next level. This will give you a place to store and record your children's progress, and the folder is great to have if you report to your local superintendent or school representative.

2. You should track what your child has learned and what they still need to learn. Here are some ways to do that:
   a) After every assignment, fill in the "Record of Progress" which follows the assignment.
   b) Fill out the "Writing Skills Mastery" as you complete assignments.
   c) Writers can always learn new things and young writers shouldn't be expected to fix all their problems right away. You can keep track of the problems you've noted but haven't yet solved using the "Spelling List" and "List of Problems to Solve."

3. Each exercise begins with a suggested time for completion. Of course, all children work at different rates. The suggested daily activities can be combined or extended depending on each child's performance and your schedule.

4. These exercises suggest that you will work with your children during the writing activity, helping them with the directions and reading what they've written. If you spend time at your children's desks or table reading what they're working on, it will serve two purposes:
   a) It will give your children constant feedback, and it will allow you to catch many writing problems before they appear in your children's final drafts.
   b) It will greatly reduce your correcting time. Most of the proofreading can be done with your children watching; so, even though your children will be writing much more than they previously have been, you should need much less preparation time for their lessons.

5. There have been enough studies done on the teaching of grammar that we must accept that, except for unusual problems such as having English as a second language, most young people have an understanding of the deep structure of their language. They might not be able to diagram their sentences or use the correct nomenclature in describing what they've written, but they were born with the gift to use words in accordance with the general rules of their language. Problems with grammar can best be solved on a need-to-know basis. The way young people learn to write is by writing and not by filling out workbooks or identifying verbs and nouns. See *Evaluating Writing* for more information on this.

6. It might be good if you don't write in this book at all but use other paper and make copies of those pages at the end of each semester's work where you can list the problems you've solved and the ones at the end of each exercise called "Record of Progress." This way your book will be completely clean for your younger brothers or sisters to use.

PRINCIPLES

The following principles were adopted by National Writing Institute before work began on *Writing Strands*. They were our guides in the initial stages of the design of the exercises.

1. Every person needs to learn to express ideas and feelings in writing.

2. There is no one right way to write anything.

3. The ability to write is not an expression of a body of knowledge that can be learned like a list of vocabulary words.

4. Writing teachers and their students both learn in any effective writing situation.

5. The product of each student's writing efforts must be seen as a success for at least the following reasons:
   a) A student in a writing situation is not in competition with anyone else.
   b) There is no perfect model against which any effort can be compared for evaluation, so there is no best way for any student to write.
   c) Every controlled writing experience will help students improve the ability to express themselves.

6. All student writing efforts are worthy of praise. The most help any writing teacher can give at any point is to show, in a positive way, what is good about a piece and how it might be improved.

7. Any writing lesson assigned, which is done independently by the student and does not have a teacher's constant feedback in the form of reinforcement and suggestions, represents a missed opportunity for the student.

8. All writing at any level is hard work, and every writer should be encouraged to feel the pride of authorship.

9. All young authors need to be published. This can be accomplished by having their work read to other family members, posted on bulletin boards (refrigerators), printed in "books" or read by other family members.

10. Students should learn that writing is fun, exciting and rewarding. This cannot be taught to a student who is punished by being made to write. Punishments, such as writing fifty times "I will not argue with my brothers," will certainly destroy the joy of learning to write.

EXERCISES * SKILLS

WRITING SKILLS MASTERY
WRITING STRANDS 2 ASSIGNMENTS

Parents: Below is a list of each assignment's objectives. As your student completes an assignment, indicate whether each objective has been met. If your child needs experience with an objective, revisit this assignment or this skill before proceeding to the next *Writing Strands* level.

Student:_____

Parent:_____ Date: _____

Skill   Needs
Mastered   Experience

Exercise #1 **WHAT IS IT?** Adjectives

_____   _____

Exercise #2 **WHAT WE DID** Listing

_____   _____

Exercise #3 **LIKE A REPORTER** Reporting

_____   _____

Exercise #4 **GOOD DEED REPORT** Paragraphing

_____   _____

Exercise #5 **MY DAY** Ordering actions

_____   _____

Exercise #6 **GROUPS** Grouping and variety

_____   _____

Exercise #7 **SMART BIRD** Story writing

_____   _____

Skill   **Needs**
Mastered   **Experience**

Exercise #8 **SELL IT**   Convincing

————   ————

Exercise #9 **INTERVIEW**   Dialogue

————   ————

Exercise #10 **DEAR FAMILY MEMBER** Letter writing

————   ————

Exercise #11 **I HELPED** Personal experience

————   ————

Exercise #12 **WHAT'S IT LIKE?** Comparison

————   ————

Exercise #13 **"HI THERE"** Greeting Cards

————   ————

Exercise #14 **ANIMALS** Role playing

————   ————

Exercise #15 **SUMMER** Imagination

————   ————

SPELLING LIST

Student Name:_____Date:_____

The research on how people learn to spell indicates that spelling mastery comes from using words. Words studied in isolation, in abstracted lists, do not carry over from the study to correct use.

This page is not to be used as a word list to be memorized. Rather it is for you to keep a record of the words your children have problems with. Turn back to this page after each exercise and record the words that you want each child to work on in the future weeks.

If you were to pick out one word a week—one that your children uses constantly—and you were to work that week with that one problem word, in two or three years your children would have mastered hundreds of words, and not have experienced the frustration of testing and failure.

You could use a large dictionary to find the derivation, study the prefixes and suffixes and the basic spelling rules that apply. If you were to make sure that that word were used correctly in all of the work that week, and from then on, you would see that spelling would improve much more than it has by studying lists of words.

You might check our book *Evaluating Writing* for more on this subject.

_____._____

_____._____

_____._____

_____._____

_____._____

_____._____

_____._____

_____._____

_____._____

_____._____

LIST OF PROBLEMS TO SOLVE

Student Name:_____Date:_____

     As you and your child work through this book, use this page as a convenient place to keep a running list of the problems you feel should be solved throughout the year.

     Keep in mind that you will have years to work with each child, and you won't be able to make any of them perfect this week or month or even this year. Record here the writing problems (for whatever reason) your child has not yet solved. If you point out to each child only one way to improve in mechanics each exercise, that would be fine. In a very few years you would have helped each child much more than you would if you were to point out everything that was wrong with each writing. Check our book *Evaluating Writing* for more on this process and why it is so very important for you and your children.

_____._____

_____._____

_____._____

_____._____

_____._____

_____._____

_____._____

_____._____

_____._____

_____._____

#1 WHAT IS IT?

ADJECTIVES

It should take you four sessions to introduce the use of adjectives. (You could use the term *descriptive words* instead of the word *adjective*.)

PREWRITING

Day One:
1. As you work through the following day-one exercise, ask your children to write the sentences you work on together.
2. Introduce a simple object to your children, like a pen or a pencil. Have your children write this sentence: *It is a pencil.*
3. Ask your children to call out in one word a description of the pencil. Your children may say a word like "Yellow" or "Long." Have them write it.
4. Ask your children to say a sentence that contains one of the adjectives descriptive of the pencil. You might hear, "It is a yellow pencil" or "It is a long pencil." Ask them to write the sentence.
5. Ask your children to say the sentence again and include two of the adjectives. Your children might say, "It's a long and yellow pencil." Remember to ask them to write each time.
6. This might be a good time to introduce to your children the idea of separating adjectives with commas. The rule that guides using commas in a series can be explained by showing that the word *and* can be used instead of a comma. If *and* can be used, a comma should go in its place.

Day Two:
1. Ask your children to write the day-one sentences so that the pronoun *it* becomes the noun *pencil*. Your children might write *The pencil is yellow*, or *The pencil is long*.
2. Prompt your children to further descriptions of the pencil by asking questions about the pencil:
   "Whose pencil is it?"
   "Where is the pencil kept?"
   "What is the pencil used for?"

   Your children should be encouraged to reply (write) in full sentences.
   It is my parent's pencil. Or, The pencil is kept in the desk.
3. Ask your children to add this information to the sentences written for day one. One part of their paper might now read:

Day one sentences:

It is a pencil.
It is a yellow pencil.
It is a long, yellow pencil.

Day two sentences:

My parent's pencil is yellow.
My parent's pencil is long.
My parent's yellow pencil is kept in the desk.

4. Ask your children to combine two adjectives in the new sentences. Your children will have to know that they can use the word and instead of a comma. The new sentences might now read like this: *My parent's pencil is long, yellow and kept in the desk.*

Day Three:
1. Ask your children to use an adjective describing you and to add this information to the sentences. When you ask them to call out adjectives about you, to save your ego, you might want to encourage your children to use adjectives like *good looking, fun, nice,* or even *wonderful.*
2. Have your children add this new description to the sentence. The sentence might now read: *My nice parent's pencil is long and yellow*

WRITING

Day Four:
1. Hold up another object. This time it should not belong to you and not be a pencil. Have your children go through the same procedure in describing this object.
2. You might ask your children to read this sentence to the rest of the family.

Remember to fill out the writing skills mastery check-off form on page iv and, if necessary, to record spelling words on page vi and other problems on page vii that you need to address in the future with your children.

Your children should now spend about a week reading and discussing ideas with you.

RECORD OF PROGRESS

Your student should fill out this page.

Name: _____ Date: _____

Exercise **#1 WHAT IS IT**

This is the best sentence I wrote this week.

_____

_____

This mistake I made this week and I will not make it next week.

_____

_____

This is the sentence that had this mistake in it.

_____

_____

This is the sentence again showing how I fixed this mistake.

_____

_____

Comments:

#2 WHAT WE DID

LISTING

It should take you four sessions to introduce the idea of listing.

PREWRITING

Day One:
1. Place a number of objects on a table. You might use such items as a pen, a pencil, a penny, a book or a ruler.
2. Ask your children to identify one of the objects, and you write its name on the board, if you have one, or on paper the children can see.
3. Have your children write the names of the objects on paper.
4. Ask your children to speak in sentences in which they list the objects. Your children might say, *There is a pen. There is a pencil. There is a penny. There is a piece of chalk. There is an eraser.* Ask your children to include all of the objects' names in one sentence.
5. Review for your children the use of commas between objects in a series. You might write a sentence on the board showing the comma placement: *On the table there are a pen, a penny, a piece of chalk and an eraser.*
6. This might be a good time to explain the choice of the use of a comma before the word *and* and the last item in a series or list.

WRITING

Day Two:
1. Put the same objects on the table again. Start the day with your children writing the sentence with the list of objects. Remind your children to separate the items with commas and give the choice to use or not to use a comma before the last item.

2. Ask your children to think about how the objects got on the table. Have your children include this information in the sentence. Your children will have to include this information in the new sentence.

It might now read: *My parent put a pen, a paper clip, a piece of chalk and an eraser on the table.* Or: *My parent put on the table a pen. . .*

3. Ask your children to collect four small things for day three. Your children should learn to spell the things they collect.

Day Three:

1. Have your children put the objects, one at a time, on a table in the middle of the room. Ask your children **to teach you** how to spell the things they brought.
2. Your children should write **four** sentences today. Each sentence should include where each object was found and what the object is. The sentences might read like these:

    I found in the hall closet and put on the table a ball.
    or;
    I got a cup from the cupboard and put it on the table.

Day Four:

1. Introduce your children to the idea of grouping objects in a listing. Have your children talk about the other members of your family. Your children should be able to group the members by age, hair color and size.
2. Have your children write a sentence about all of your family members. You will have to start your children off with the beginning of the sentence:

    Of the members in our family, two have blond hair. . . or There are two members with blond hair, thirteen with brown hair and six with very dark. . .

Remember to fill out the writing skills mastery check-off form on page iv and, if necessary, to record spelling words on page vi and other problems on page vii that you need to address in the future with your children.

Your children should now spend about a week reading and discussing ideas with you.

RECORD OF PROGRESS

Your student should fill out this page.

Name: _____ Date: _____

Exercise **#2 WHAT WE DID**

This is the best sentence I wrote this week.

_____

_____

This mistake I made this week and I will not make it next week.

_____

_____

This is the sentence that had this mistake in it.

_____

_____

This is the sentence again showing how I fixed this mistake.

_____

_____

Comments:

#3 LIKE A REPORTER

REPORTING

It should take you four sessions to introduce reporting.

PREWRITING

Day One:
1. You might want to talk to your children about reporting: where it is done, by whom and what it's like. You could talk about the different kinds of reporters there are, like newspaper and TV reporters, child protection workers, scientists and policemen.

2. Explain what will happen on day two to give your children a chance to think about what kind of reporting might be done.

Day Two:
1. Yesterday you explained that there would be a chance to report on an exciting event. One of your family members will have to play a part in this activity. If you don't have a volunteer for this part, you might ask a neighbor to help.

2. Your children should "hide" in the living room and watch the "subject" come into the room and do a "good deed." This can be cleaning the room, bringing flowers as a gift, or any other nice act. This person will then leave the room or house.

3. You should have your children verbally list the events witnessed. This should be done in the order the events happened. Your children will have a tendency to omit some of the events. There will be a tendency to "report" that Mrs. Jones brought the flowers and put them on the hall table. Insist that the details be included.

4. Ask your children what the first action was that they saw, then ask what was the next, and so on. These actions should be numbered.

The responses might sound like this:

1) The door opened.
2) Mrs Jones looked in the room.
3) Mrs. Jones came in the room.
4) Mrs. Jones looked around the room.
5) Mrs. Jones had flowers in her hand.
6) Mrs. Jones walked over to the hall table.
7) Mrs. Jones put the vase of flowers on the table.
8) Mrs. Jones arranged the flowers so they were pretty.
9) Mrs. Jones left the room.
10) Mrs. Jones closed the door.

WRITING

Days Three and Four:

1. Your children should write at the top of the page "Good Deed Report," or "Newspaper Story." Encourage them to put in the report all of the details noticed on day two. The listing made on day two can now be written. Ask to have the listing written in full sentences. The report's events should not be numbered or written in list form.

2. If your children choose to write the report as if it were to be for a newspaper, your children then could write headlines:

GOOD DEED DONE IN LOCAL HOME
or

LOCAL REPORTER WATCHES GOOD DEED

Remember to fill out the writing skills mastery check-off form on page iv and, if necessary, to record spelling words on page vi and other problems on page vii that you need to address in the future with your children.

Your children should now spend about a week reading and discussing ideas with you.

RECORD OF PROGRESS

Your student should fill out this page.

Name: _____ Date: _____

Exercise **#3 LIKE A REPORTER**

This is the best sentence I wrote this week.

_____

_____

This mistake I made this week and I will not make it next week.

_____

_____

This is the sentence that had this mistake in it.

_____

_____

This is the sentence again showing how I fixed this mistake.

_____

_____

Comments:

#4 GOOD DEED REPORT

PARAGRAPHING

It should take you four days to introduce paragraphing.

PREWRITING

Day One:

1. If your children did not finish the third exercise, they should be encouraged to copy the omitted items.

2. Introduce your children to the idea of a paragraph as found in a report. They should know that the first sentence identifies three things: the place, the time and the event. The rest of the paragraph should consist of the details.

   This first sentence can be done orally. Your children should be able to speak a sentence with those three conditions in it. Then they should write this sentence above the list on the paper they wrote for the last exercise, "Report."

This sentence above "Report" might now read:

> *On Tuesday, in my front room, Mrs. Jones did a good deed.*

> *The door opened. Mrs. Jones looked in the room. Mrs. Jones sneaked into the room. Mrs. Jones looked around and saw the hall table. Mrs. Jones had flowers in her hands. Mrs. Jones put the flowers and the vase on the hall table. Mrs. Jones arranged the flowers so they were pretty. Mrs. Jones left the house. The door closed.*

WRITING

Day Two:

1. Introduce your children to pronouns. If you were to read your children's papers to them, they would hear a lot of *Mrs. Jones's* in them.
2. Have your children rewrite the sentences using *she* in place of *Mrs. Jones* after the second sentence.

Days Three and Four:

1. Have your children look at the paper they wrote for the second exercise, "Listing." They combined items in sentences. They can combine actions for this exercise in the same way.

2. You will have to talk your children through this combining exercise before they begin to write. You might have your children combine two actions in each sentence. Their papers might now read like this:

On Tuesday, in the front room of my house, Mrs. Jones did a good deed. The door opened and Mrs. Jones looked in the room. She sneaked into the room and looked around. She saw the hall table and put a vase of flowers on it. She arranged the flowers so they were pretty and then opened the outside door and left the house.

Remember to fill out the writing skills mastery check-off form on page iv and, if necessary, to record spelling words on page vi and other problems on page vii that you need to address in the future with your children.

Your children should now spend about a week reading and discussing ideas with you.

RECORD OF PROGRESS

Your student should fill out this page.

Name: _____ Date: _____

Exercise **#4 GOOD DEED REPORT**

This is the best sentence I wrote this week.

_____

_____

This mistake I made this week and I will not make it next week.

_____

_____

This is the sentence that had this mistake in it.

_____

_____

This is the sentence again showing how I fixed this mistake.

_____

_____

Comments:

#5 MY DAY

ORDERING ACTIONS

It should take you four sessions to introduce the idea of ordering actions.

PREWRITING

Day One:

    1. Write on the board the order of the way you have organized your children's day: reading, spelling, arithmetic and so on.

    2. Ask each of your children to speak a sentence that includes one of the subjects. You should hear:

        "I study reading."
        "I study spelling."
        "I study arithmetic."

    3. Ask your children to write a sentence for each of the subjects studied during the day. Have your children include free time or lunch break.

    4. Ask your children to be sure to know how to spell the numbers that will be used on day two: *first, second, third* and so on.

WRITING

Day Two:

    1. Ask your children to write the numbers they learned for today on the board or on a piece of paper or to spell them out loud and you can write them on the board.

    2. Ask your children to rewrite the day-one sentences so they include the order of the activities. The paper might now read:

        First, I study reading.   *Third, I study arithmetic.*
        Second, I study spelling.   *Fourth, I have free time.*

Day Three:

    1. Talk about feelings to your children. Your children should understand that all people have feelings about everything they do. Your children should have emotional reactions to daily activities. They should feel differently about free time than they do about spelling. Your children should see that this is the way it should be and should not feel guilty about enjoying one activity more than any other one. You might have your children talk about how they feel when they have to help you and they would rather be playing, or when they can't do something they want to do.

    2. Ask your children to put after each of the sentences a word that tells how they feel about that activity. The paper might now read:

        1. First, I study reading. Blah
        2. Second, I study spelling. Fun
        3. Third, I study arithmetic. Hard
        4. Fourth, I have free time. Great

Day Four:

    1. Ask your children to rewrite the day-three sentences to include how they feel about the activities. The complete sentences might now read:

        1. First, I study reading, which is a blah time.
        2. Second, I study spelling, which is fun.
        3. Third, I study arithmetic and I think it is hard.
        4. Fourth, I have free time, which is great.

Remember to fill out the writing skills mastery check-off form on page iv and, if necessary, to record spelling words on page vi and other problems on page vii that you need to address in the future with your children.

Your children should now spend about a week reading and discussing ideas with you.

RECORD OF PROGRESS

Your student should fill out this page.

Name: _____ Date: _____

Exercise **#5 MY DAY**

This is the best sentence I wrote this week.

_____

_____

This mistake I made this week and I will not make it next week.

_____

_____

This is the sentence that had this mistake in it.

_____

_____

This is the sentence again showing how I fixed this mistake.

_____

_____

Comments:

#6 GROUPS

GROUPING AND VARIETY

It should take you four sessions to introduce the grouping of ideas or items and the creating of variety in sentence structure.

PREWRITING

Day One:
1. In lesson five your children wrote seven or eight sentences that sound like this: *The eighth thing I study is geography which is fun.*
2. If your children followed directions, all the sentences will sound the same. Your children need to learn to put variety in the structuring of sentences. This can be accomplished if they combine what they learned in lesson two and three: "Listing" and "Reporting." You might review those two lessons with your children.

Day Two:
1. Ask your children to mark pieces of paper into three equal sections by drawing two vertical lines from the top of the page to the bottom.
2. They should label these three columns: LIKE, OKAY and DO NOT LIKE.
3. The subjects your children wrote about in exercise number five should then be listed with the times they occur under the headings that represent how they feel about them. It will help your children to understand this if you show your children on the board how this will look.

Each child's paper might now look like this:

Like	*Okay*	*Do not like*
3 Spelling	*1 Reading*	*2 Arithmetic*
4 Recess	*7 Geography*	
5 Lunch	*6 Science*	
8 Free time		

WRITING

Days Three and Four:

1. Your children will now have three groups of studies to write about instead of six or seven individual ones. Ask your children to combine the sentences so that they write in the first sentence about the studies they "like." Your children should include in this sentence the periods when they studies those subjects.

    The first sentence might read: *I like spelling, free time and lunch best, which are my third, fourth and fifth classes.*

2. The next sentence should include the studies your children feel "okay" about. It should be structured differently from the first sentence. You may have to show your children two or three ways to change the structuring. It might read: *Reading, geography and science are my first, seventh and sixth subjects and they are okay,* or, *Reading, geography and science, my first, seventh and sixth subjects are okay.*

3. Your children should write the third sentence using a different structure. It might read: *I do not like arithmetic which I study second.* Or: *The second thing I study is arithmetic, which I do not like.*

Remember to fill out the writing skills mastery check-off form on page iv and, if necessary, to record spelling words on page vi and other problems on page vii that you need to address in the future with your children.

Your children should now spend about a week reading and discussing ideas with you.

RECORD OF PROGRESS

Your student should fill out this page.

Name: _____ Date: _____

Exercise **#6 GROUPS**

This is the best sentence I wrote this week.

_____

_____

This mistake I made this week and I will not make it next week.

_____

_____

This is the sentence that had this mistake in it.

_____

_____

This is the sentence again showing how I fixed this mistake.

_____

_____

Comments:

#7 SMART BIRD

STORY WRITING

It should take you four sessions to introduce the idea of story writing.

PREWRITING

Day One:

1. You should introduce the idea that all stories have at least one main character. Your children should understand that this character is the one the story is about.
   a) This character will have a problem.
   b) This character will have to solve the problem.

2. You might want to make some stories up, and you could have your children be the main characters. You could ask your children to suggest ways the characters could solve the problems.

Day Two:

1. Ask your children to write about Tom, a turkey who hid at Thanksgiving time.

   Your children will have to decide for this story:
   a) Why Tom hid
   b) Where Tom hid
   c) When Tom came out from hiding
   d) What the farmer did or thought when he saw Tom after Thanksgiving Day

2. You might want to ask your children to talk about these four writing problems before they start to write.

This conversation with your children might sound like this one.

When writers write stories, they can have lots of things happen that could never happen in real life. In a story about a family of rabbits, the author might have the rabbits talk together. We know that rabbits don't speak English, but this is okay for a story. In our story about a turkey at Thanksgiving, we could have the turkeys be very smart if we wanted to. Let's figure out some of the things that Tom, the turkey, might think if he were smart:

1. Would Tom know what Thanksgiving was all about?
2. Would Tom know that Thanksgiving is dangerous for turkeys?
3. Where would Tom hide on a farm?
4. When would Tom come out from hiding?
5. What would the farmer do for dinner if he couldn't find Tom?

WRITING

Days Three and Four:

1. Your children should start the story. You might suggest a beginning for the story that would identify the time, place and character. It might read: *Tom lived on a farm. Tom hid three days before Thanksgiving. Tom was a turkey.*

2. Now have your children combine these three sentences as they learned to do in exercise six so that they might now read: *Tom, a turkey, hid on the farm, where he lived, three days before Thanksgiving.* Or, you could demonstrate how to rearrange the wording in the sentence: *Three days before Thanksgiving, a turkey named Tom hid on the farm where he lived.*

3. Your children should then work through the above five questions. After the beginning sentences, the story can be written in as few as ten more sentences. But, you might encourage your children to use as much detail as they can manage.

4. Your children might want to illustrate the story with pictures of Tom hiding from the farmer. These could be drawn or cut from magazines. A collage might be fun.

5. If you have a student who likes to write and can handle a more complicated exercise, you might suggest a description of the meatless dinner the farmer's family ate that Thanksgiving Day.

Remember to fill out the writing skills mastery check-off form on page iv and, if necessary, to record spelling words on page vi and other problems on page vii that you need to address in the future with your children.

Your children should now spend about a week reading and discussing ideas with you.

RECORD OF PROGRESS

Your student should fill out this page.

Name: _____ Date: _____

Exercise **#7 SMART BIRD**

This is the best sentence I wrote this week.

_____

_____

This mistake I made this week and I will not make it next week.

_____

_____

This is the sentence that had this mistake in it.

_____

_____

This is the sentence again showing how I fixed this mistake.

_____

_____

Comments:

#8 SELL IT

CONVINCING

It should take you eight sessions to introduce the ideas involved in convincing others.

PREWRITING

Prior to day one, your children should be introduced to radio or TV advertisements—who puts them on the air waves, why they are on and why they are effective. They should know that there are limits to what they should believe in these advertisements.

Day One:
1. It will help the understanding of what you want done if you advertise something in the room for your children, much as it would be advertised on television or radio. It could be something simple, such as a new pencil, ball-point pen or a book.

2. Your children will prepare their own advertisements and will have to:

   a) Choose a product to sell
   b) Present the product to a TV or radio audience
   c) Mention the good characteristics of the product
   d) Ask the audience to buy the product

Day Two:
1. Your children should bring to this lesson products they are going to "sell." They should be small objects that are easy to manipulate.

WRITING
2. Your children should list the good characteristics of the products. This list can read like the example below:

Billy Ball-Point Pen

1) The pen is pretty.　　　　　*3) The pen is cheap.*
2) The pen writes with dark ink.　　*4) The pen is strong.*

Those characteristics on the previous page should then be written into sentences that are not all alike.

Day Three:

1. Your children should write the last part of the advertisement, the part where they ask the audience to buy the product. This can read: *So, the next time you're in a store, pick up a Billy Ball-Point Pen.*

2. Your children should write the parts of the advertisement where they show the audience that there is a need for the product.

   If this is a TV ad, it doesn't need to be presented only in dialogue. It can be in actions. In the case of the ball-point pen advertisement, your children could write: *The talent (actor) will try to write with a pen that doesn't work.*

3. If you have your children fold their papers once vertically down the middle, they can have a script that they can give to the actors. It could start like this:

See and/or Hear	Actor
Music (tape recorders work)	Tries to write with pen that doesn't work.
Gets idea - takes B pen from pocket	B pen works. *This is a Billy Ball-Point Pen. . .*

Day Four:

Your children should practice producing this advertisement. For some advertisements your children might need to work with another person. In this case there would be the producer (writer) and the talent (actor).

Days Five through Eight:

When your children produce the advertisement for the family, they might do so from inside or behind a large cardboard carton (One that a refrigerator came from works well). The front can be cut out so the box looks like a radio or a TV set. Some students might like to make the set by cutting the hole and drawing the controls on the cardboard.

Remember to fill out the writing skills mastery check-off form on page iv and, if necessary, to record spelling words on page vi and other problems on page vii that you need to address in the future with your children.

Your children should now spend about a week reading and discussing ideas with you.

RECORD OF PROGRESS

Your student should fill out this page.

Name: _____ Date: _____

Exercise **#8 SELL IT**

This is the best sentence I wrote this week.

_____

_____

This mistake I made this week and I will not make it next week.

_____

_____

This is the sentence that had this mistake in it.

_____

_____

This is the sentence again showing how I fixed this mistake.

_____

_____

Comments:

#9 INTERVIEW

DIALOGUE

It should take you four sessions to introduce the writing of dialogue.

PREWRITING

Day One:
Review a few of the main rules of punctuation in dialogue. You might write these five examples on the chalkboard or a piece of scrap paper. Your children should learn them.

1) End punctuation marks should be within the quotation marks.

Bill said, "Help me (.)"

2) What a character does should be separated from what that character says by a comma.

Bill ran into the room and said(,) "Help me."

3) What the character says should begin with a capital letter.

Bill said, "(H)elp me."

4) What the character says does not end with a period unless what the character says is at the end of the whole sentence.

"Help me(,)" Bill said.

5) Each new speaker starts a new paragraph.

( )Bill said, "Help me."
( )His mother said to her child, "Bill, why are you always asking for help?"
( )Bill said, "I need a lot of attention."

An easy way to show your children these rules in operation is to take any novel or story that has dialogue in it and together find examples of the rules. These rules are very standard and your children must learn to use them.

Day Two:

1. Your children will write an interview that they will have with a non-person, such as a dog, cat or bike. They can "talk" to trees, flowers or family cars. They will have to imagine what a non-person might say to them.

2. You might show your children how this works by pretending you are interviewing your desk or couch. Just for fun, one of the other family members or a neighbor can be hidden under the desk or behind the couch when the interview starts. (You will have to set this up on day one.) If you get your children near the desk when you're explaining what an interview is, the effect of the desk talking back might be a fun surprise. This demonstration interview might go like this:

   "Hello, Desk. Are you ready to go to work?"
   "Yes."
   "What? I didn't hear you."
   "I'm ready to do whatever you want me to do."
   "Are my pencils all sharp?"
   "You'll have to ask the pencil sharpener."
   "I can't. The pencil sharpener was made in Japan and it can't speak English."

3. Talk to your children about what might be felt and said by a tree, a flower or a dog. If you ask your children the following questions, it might help their imaginations. (Notice that the questions are open ended—they cannot be answered with a yes or no.)

   a) Why does a tree like rain?
   b) What does a tree do when it is lonely?
   c) What do trees talk together about?
   d) What do trees eat when they get hungry?
   e) What questions has this tree wanted to ask a person?

WRITING

Day Three:

1. The interview paper should start with an introduction that explains who or what was interviewed. This introduction might read like this:

   I interviewed my dog last night. I asked her some questions. I asked, "What have you done today?" My dog raised her head off of her paws, yawned and said, "Not much. I just stayed in the house and took a lot of naps."

2. The body of the interview should contain the details of the conversation your children had with this "friend." In some cases it might be necessary for you to play the object being interviewed to give your children some practice. If this is done, then, when it is time to conduct the interview for this exercise, they will be able to play both parts with confidence.

It might help to use a tape recorder on some of the practice interviews. This will give your children an opportunity to review their work and develop their interviewing techniques.

Day Four:
Another day might be needed to work on punctuation.

Remember to fill out the writing skills mastery check-off form on page iv and, if necessary, to record spelling words on page vi and other problems on page vii that you need to address in the future with your children.

Your children should now spend about a week reading and discussing ideas with you.

RECORD OF PROGRESS

Your student should fill out this page.

Name: _____ Date: _____

Exercise **#9 INTERVIEW**

This is the best sentence I wrote this week.

_____

_____

This mistake I made this week and I will not make it next week.

_____

_____

This is the sentence that had this mistake in it.

_____

_____

This is the sentence again showing how I fixed this mistake.

_____

_____

Comments:

#10 DEAR FAMILY MEMBER

LETTER WRITING

It should take you five sessions to introduce letter writing.

PREWRITING

Day One:
1. You might talk to your children about the idea of giving gifts on birthdays. You could introduce some family story about your children's birth dates. You might explain why all people do not celebrate birthdays as your family does. I'm sure that your children understand the idea of gift giving, but you might introduce some religious and cultural background for the custom.

2. Your children will be writing a letter to some family member. In a common, traditional letter, the one containing a list of wanted toys, children ask for gifts for themselves. In the letter your children will write, they will:
   a) Ask for a gift for a person they love.
   b) Tell what they have done to the person about whom they wrote to the family member and include a copy of their letter to that family member. This then will be a letter within a letter. More on this process later.

3. Your children should prepare for day one:
   a) The correct spelling of the name of the person to whom they are writing (see days two and three)
   b) That person's address
   c) An idea for a gift

4. You might put on the board the format of a friendly letter and have your children copy it or you might duplicate it for your children.

WRITING

Days Two and Three:
Your children will write the letter to another family member asking for a special gift for a person they love. Show your children this list of what the letter might include:

1. Who the gift is to be for and what it is to be
2. That person's address
3. A statement that that person is loved
4. The fact that that person needs or wants the gift

An example of how the body of this letter might read should help:

> *I would like you to give a new can opener to my grandmother. Her name is Mrs. Owens. She lives at 222 Oak Street, Midtown, Ohio 43909.*
> *I love my grandmother very much and want her to have a good birthday. She needs a new can opener because her old one does not work so well. She has to jiggle the plug all the time to make it run.*

Days Four and Five:

1. Your children will write letters to the people they asked to have the gift sent to and include in it the letter to the other family member. You might ask your children to prepare envelopes. You might write the address of the person to receive the letter or show your children how to look the addresses up in the phone book.

2. This letter should explain the writing of the original letter to the other family member and should include the following ideas:

   a) The exercise of writing a request for a gift letter to a family member
   b) The reasons for this letter (. . .because I love you and I know you need this gift)
   c) The hope that the other family member will get the letter and send the right gift

The letter explaining the exercise might read:

Dear Grandma,

> *I wrote to (family member). I am sending you a copy of this letter. I love you and I know you would like this gift. I hope (the family member) gives you the can opener.*

> *Happy Birthday,*

Remember to fill out the writing skills mastery check-off form on page iv and, if necessary, to record spelling words on page vi and other problems on page vii that you need to address in the future with your children.

Your children should now spend about a week reading and discussing ideas with you.

RECORD OF PROGRESS

Your student should fill out this page.

Name: _____ Date: _____

Exercise **#10 DEAR FAMILY MEMBER**

This is the best sentence I wrote this week.

_____

_____

This mistake I made this week and I will not make it next week.

_____

_____

This is the sentence that had this mistake in it.

_____

_____

This is the sentence again showing how I fixed this mistake.

_____

_____

Comments:

#11 I HELPED

PERSONAL EXPERIENCE

It should take you five sessions to introduce personal narration.

PREWRITING

Day One:

1. You might introduce your children to the idea of autobiographies. You could explain who writes them and why they are written—to make money, to tell the writer's side of a story, or to entertain. You could mention some famous people who have written in this form. You could suggest that an autobiography is a series of events in the writer's life. Your children will not be writing actual autobiographies, but a similar exercise—writing of a personal event or experience.

2. There should be some structure to the writing. The following may help. They should base this writing on an event when they had opportunities to help someone else. You might write this list out for your children. The writing should include:

   a) When this event occurred
   b) Who they helped
   c) Why they did this for that person
   d) What they did to help
   e) How they felt about the event when they were done helping

WRITING

3. Your children can start this paper today with point (a). Your children should be encouraged to write with detail. The first sentences could read:

   Last summer I stayed for two weeks with my uncle on his farm. I didn't want to go. I knew I would miss my friends.

Days Two through Five:

1. If they prefer, your children could change the order from the suggested order of the list of what to include in this paper. In some cases it might make more sense to tell the reader why they helped before telling about who they helped.

2. Most of your children's papers should be taken up with explanations of what they did to help. Encourage your children to use a good bit of detail in this section. There might be a paragraph or two just about this part. It might help your children to structure section (d) if you give them this example to follow. They should number and list the steps they took to help—it can look like the example below:

   1) I got the tool box out of the garage.
   2) I opened the box near where my dad was working.
   3) I waited for him to ask me to hand him a tool.
   4) Each time he asked for a tool, I handed it to him.
   5) When the car was fixed, I wiped off the tools.
   6) The last thing I did was put the box away in the garage.

3. To give your children encouragement in writing with detail, which most students need, you might have your children talk through the list of actions they took in helping someone. If you work them through this verbalization, it should help them see what is meant by your request for detail.

4. When your children reach the last part of the list of events (e), they could explain how this experience of helping someone changed how they felt about doing it. They could then refer their readers back to section (c) where they explain how their feelings changed.

   This part of your children's papers might read:

   When my dad first asked me to help him, I was happy to do it, but I didn't think it would be fun. When we were done fixing the car, I realized I had had fun, and I was glad I had helped.

Remember to fill out the writing skills mastery check-off form on page iv and, if necessary, to record spelling words on page vi and other problems on page vii that you need to address in the future with your children.

Your children should now spend about a week reading and discussing ideas with you.

RECORD OF PROGRESS

Your student should fill out this page.

Name: _____ Date: _____

Exercise **#11 I HELPED**

This is the best sentence I wrote this week.

_____

_____

This mistake I made this week and I will not make it next week.

_____

_____

This is the sentence that had this mistake in it.

_____

_____

This is the sentence again showing how I fixed this mistake.

_____

_____

Comments:

#12 WHAT'S IT LIKE?

COMPARISON

It should take you four days to introduce the techniques of comparison.

PREWRITING

Day One:

Most people have trouble describing objects in isolation. This is especially true for young children. They have a very limited basis for the establishment of adequate understandings of characteristics. A child's feelings of frustration can be well understood by those of us who were brought up before the metric system was introduced in the schools in this country. I still have to translate in my mind before I can understand distances given in meters, or kilometers.

Your children might like to know that adults still have trouble understanding some relationships. You might put some objects on a desk and ask your children to describe them using relationships. Any group of objects will work. An apple, an eraser, a pencil, a paper bag, a book, and a small box would be fine.

Ask your children to describe one of the objects only in relationship to the other objects. It's not enough for a child to describe the chalk as white. They would have to call its color lighter than the paper bag, even lighter in color than the dust on the eraser. The shine of the chalk's color would have to be referred to as duller than the shine of the color of the apple. This gets complicated and your children should have fun with it.

WRITING

Days Two Through Four:

1. Put five new objects on the desk. Your children will have to describe in writing one of them using only the other four objects as references. They can't say the banana is about eight inches long unless there is such a thing as an inch on the desk. They can't say the banana is soft. They must say that the banana is softer than one or more of the other objects.
2. Your children should be able to pick which object they want to describe. They will be able to talk about that one object only by referring to the characteristics of the other four objects.

3. You might make a list of the characteristics of the object of your children's choice. They can then describe the object by comparing its characteristics with the following characteristics of the other objects.

     A) Color
     1) Darkness
     2) Lightness
     3) Shade

     B) Shape
     1) Roundness
     2) Sharpness
     3) Bumpiness

     C) Size
     1) Length
     2) Depth
     3) Width
     4) Height

Your children might have trouble limiting themselves only to referring to the other objects. You may have to spend the second day doing nothing but reading their efforts and pointing out the restrictions of the exercise.

Remember to fill out the writing skills mastery check-off form on page iv and, if necessary, to record spelling words on page vi and other problems on page vii that you need to address in the future with your children.

Your children should now spend about a week reading and discussing ideas with you.

RECORD OF PROGRESS

Your student should fill out this page.

Name: _____ Date: _____

Exercise **#12 WHAT'S IT LIKE**

This is the best sentence I wrote this week.

_____

_____

This mistake I made this week and I will not make it next week.

_____

_____

This is the sentence that had this mistake in it.

_____

_____

This is the sentence again showing how I fixed this mistake.

_____

_____

Comments:

#13 "HI THERE"

GREETING CARDS

It should take you four days to introduce the making of greeting cards.

PREWRITING

Day One:

Many people your children's ages have been playing with rhyming for two or three years in their games and in the books they've read. Most students like the sounds of rhyming words and this exercise should be fun for them.

1. Give your children the assignment to bring ten small objects to the lesson on day one. You might suggest stuffed animals, cut-out figures, small toys, pieces of fruit and pictures from magazines.

2. You can hold up one of the objects and have your children see if they can find another object or a part of something that rhymes with it. If you hold up a nickel, your children might be able to find a picture of a pickle. If your children cannot find a rhyming object, you might suggest the names of objects that would rhyme with it.

WRITING

Day Two:

1. Your children will write verses and draw the illustrations for greeting cards. These can be special day cards or just "I miss you" cards.

2. Show your children how to fold a piece of paper into quarters so that it looks like a greeting card.

3. Your children could compose verses (which should rhyme if they can manage this) before they write in their cards. This will give you a chance to help.

These verses can be short and quite simple. A good exercise might be to copy some from the card display at the drug store.

Your children will be encouraged by simple examples such as:

I was thinking of you
Because I was blue.

This card is to tell you
I like you.

I am thinking about you.

4. Your public library should have a rhyming dictionary. You can show your children how to find rhymes and then ask them to look up words for their rhymes. If this is too hard for them, you should do it for them.

5. Rhyming is very hard for some people. If your children find this impossible to do, you might take a field trip to the card shop for some examples of cards that don't rhyme. Many of the "funny" cards do not.

Day Three:

Your children should illustrate their cards. If you have an older child who has some artistic ability who could help, that could be fun. You might want to set aside two or three extra days and ask the older child to demonstrate types of illustrations and various media for the pictures.

Day Four:

Your children should print their text or verse cards. You might show your children how to draw faint pencil lines on the card paper so they can have straight lines of print. Your children might like to send their cards to friends or a member of your family.

Remember to fill out the writing skills mastery check-off form on page iv and, if necessary, to record spelling words on page vi and other problems on page vii that you need to address in the future with your children.

Your children should now spend about a week reading and discussing ideas with you.

RECORD OF PROGRESS

Your student should fill out this page.

Name: _____ Date: _____

Exercise #13 "HI THERE"

This is the best sentence I wrote this week.

_____

_____

This mistake I made this week and I will not make it next week.

_____

_____

This is the sentence that had this mistake in it.

_____

_____

This is the sentence again showing how I fixed this mistake.

_____

_____

Comments:

#14 ANIMALS

ROLE PLAYING

It should take you six sessions to give an experience in role playing.

PREWRITING

Day One:
1. Children spend a lot of time daydreaming, and the people who study child development think they should and that this is good. You might tell your children about daydreams and how much good has come from them. You might mention Edison, Einstein and Fulton. To dream is to create—in the mind.

2. To give your children the feeling that it's good to daydream and that all people do it, you might tell your children about one of your daydreams, or you could use some of the old standbys: *If I had a million dollars. . . If I were a king. . . If I were a great hunter. . . If I were the smartest person in the world. . . If I were the most popular person in the town . . .* and, *If I were a great baseball or football player.* You might suggest that many daydreams begin with the word, *If.*

3. Your children might not want to talk about their daydreams, but they might be willing to talk about the daydreams of one of their friends.

Day Two:
1. It might help your children to begin to understand the feelings an animal might have if you were to act out the characteristics of an animal. A cat is an easy one to do.

2. Your children might like to "become" an animal and let you guess which one.

WRITING

Days Three through Six:
1. Your children will write a description of this animal in list form. This means that the items on the list will not have to be in sentences. They can use just words or phrases if they like. You might make a list or duplicate the one on the next page to help your children get organized in their role playing. Here are some suggestions for items for your children's list:

ANIMAL NAME

1. Looks Like:
a) Eyes
b) Hair
c) Feet
d) Tail

2. Moves Like:
a) Walks
b) Sits
c) Lies down
d) Chews or eats
e) Swallows
f) Gulps

3. Sounds Like:
a) Roars
b) Whines
c) Purrs
d) Barks

4. Feels Like:
a) Slick
b) Furry
c) Wet
d) Rough

2. Your children's papers might start with: *If I had been created to be an animal, I would most like to be a. . . .*

3. The rest of each paper can describe any part of the life of that animal. Your children can write about what that animal would:

1) Think
2) Do
3) Want
4) Fear
5) Eat
6) Hope for

Remember to fill out the writing skills mastery check-off form on page iv and, if necessary, to record spelling words on page vi and other problems on page vii that you need to address in the future with your children.

Your children should now spend about a week reading and discussing ideas with you.

RECORD OF PROGRESS

Your student should fill out this page.

Name: _____ Date: _____

Exercise **#14 ANIMALS**

This is the best sentence I wrote this week.

_____

_____

This mistake I made this week and I will not make it next week.

_____

_____

This is the sentence that had this mistake in it.

_____

_____

This is the sentence again showing how I fixed this mistake.

_____

_____

Comments:

#15 SUMMER!

IMAGINATION

It should take your children many sessions to write this last paper.

PREWRITING

Day One:

Start this exercise by telling your children what you would like to do this coming summer. Make your wish fanciful and imaginative to encourage your children to do likewise. Ask your children what they would like to do this summer if they could do anything they would like. You and they should not be restricted to what is possible.

To give your children the idea of this exercise, you might start by telling your children about boarding your airplane and flying to the coast where you have your yacht and starting your cruise around the world.

WRITING

Day Two:

1. In this exercise your children should write in past tense. You will have to explain that it is now next fall and they are writing the first paper in the third level. Your children will be writing about what they did in the summer between second and third levels. The paper might begin: *Last summer I...*

2. Your children should follow some outline. Write this one out or duplicate it.

TITLE

Introduction

    First three sentences
    a) What I did or where I went
    b) Who went with me
    c) How long the trip lasted

Body (3 parts)

Paragraph 1
a) What I always wanted to do
b) When I started
c) How I could do this (money or time)

Paragraph 2 (work for details)
a) What I did
b) What I saw
c) What it was like

Paragraph 3
a) What happened to me
b) What this made me think and feel like
c) Why I liked this

Conclusion
a) How I feel about the summer
b) I would or would not like to do it again
c) What my parents thought

Days Three though the end of the Exercise:

This can be as long and as involved an exercise as you want it to be. Your children can work with other members of the family and illustrate this paper with pictures (drawn or cut from magazines) that they "took" while they were having their trip.

Your children can spend time in the library looking up the places they visited. They can study some of the activities they engaged in. You can even take field trips to talk to people about travel.

There might be a travel agency in your area that would allow an agent to take the time to talk about different places. This agent might give your children posters, brochures and maps of different countries and resorts that your children could cut up and use for illustrations or hang on the board or use for their "photo" albums.

Remember to fill out the writing skills mastery check-off form on page iv and, if necessary, to record spelling words on page vi and other problems on page vii that you need to address in the future with your children.

Your children should now spend about a week reading and discussing ideas with you.

RECORD OF PROGRESS

Your student should fill out this page.

Name: _____ Date: _____

Exercise **#15 SUMMER!**

This is the best sentence I wrote this week.

_____

_____

This mistake I made this week and I will not make it next week.

_____

_____

This is the sentence that had this mistake in it.

_____

_____

This is the sentence again showing how I fixed this mistake.

_____

_____

Comments:

FINAL COMMENT ON *WRITING STRANDS LEVEL 2*

At this point, the end of your child's first year of writing training in *Writing Strands*, you should have, on page vii, a list of problems to solve next year when you work with *Writing Strands 3*. You also have a spelling list that you can work with this summer.

This year you worked closely with your child, reading the exercises aloud and explaining what to do, but that must change. Children have to be weaned from that kind of help. *Writing Strands 3* is written for the child to work in alone. But, you will be needed to encourage and help your child overcome writing problems. The book *Evaluating Writing* can save you time and will save your child much pain.

Continue working with your children introducing to them the joys of communication. Make sure they see you reading and sharing your ideas with the rest of your family. They will copy your attitudes and your actions.

To place your *Writing Strands* order, simply fill out this form and send it to us by mail or by fax. If you would like to get your order started even faster, go to the *Writing Strands* website and place your order online at: www.writingstrands.com

		QTY	Total
Writing Strands 1 Oral Work for ages 3-8	$14.95 ea.	___	_____
Writing Strands 2 About 7 years old	$18.95 ea.	___	_____
Writing Strands 3 Starting program ages 8-12	$18.95 ea.	___	_____
Writing Strands 4 Any age after Level 3 or starting program at age 13 or 14	$18.95 ea.	___	_____
Writing Strands 5 Any age after Level 4 or starting program at age 15 or 16	$20.95 ea.	___	_____
Writing Strands 6 17 or any age after Level 5	$20.95 ea.	___	_____
Writing Strands 7 18 or any age after Level 6	$22.95 ea.	___	_____
Writing Exposition Senior high school and after Level 7	$22.95 ea.	___	_____
Creating Fiction Senior high school and after Level 7	$22.95 ea.	___	_____
Evaluating Writing Parents' manual for all levels of *Writing Strands*	$19.95 ea.	___	_____
Reading Strands Parents' manual for story and book interpretation, all grades	$22.95 ea.	___	_____
Communication and Interpersonal Relationships Communication Manners (teens)	$17.95 ea.	___	_____
Basic Starter Set (SAVE $5.00) *Writing Strands 2, Writing Strands 3, Reading Strands* and *Evaluating Writing*	$75.80 per set	___	_____
Intermediate Starter Set (SAVE $10.00) *Writing Strands 3, Writing Strands 4, Evaluating Writing, Communication and Interpersonal Relationships* and *Reading Strands*	$88.75 per set	___	_____
Advanced Starter Set (SAVE $30.00) *Writing Strands 5, Writing Strands 6, Writing Strands 7, Writing Exposition, Creating Fiction, Evaluating Writing, Communication and Interpersonal Relationships* and *Reading Strands*	$138.60 per set	___	_____
Dragonslaying Is for Dreamers – Package 1st novel in *Dragonslaying* trilogy (Early teens) and parents' manual for analyzing the novel.	$18.95 ea.	___	_____
Dragonslaying Is for Dreamers Novel only	$9.95 ea.	___	_____
Axel Meets the Blue Men 2nd novel in *Dragonslaying* trilogy (Teens)	$9.95 ea.	___	_____
Axel's Challenge Final novel in *Dragonslaying* trilogy (Teens)	$9.95 ea.	___	_____
Dragonslaying Trilogy All three novels in series	$25.00 set	___	_____
Dragonslaying Trilogy and Parents' Manual Three novels plus parents' manual for first novel	$32.99 set	___	_____

SUBTOTAL (use this total to calculate shipping) _____

Texas residents: Add 8.25% sales tax _____

U.S. Shipping: $6 for orders up to $75 _____

$8 for orders over $75 _____

Outside U.S. Shipping: $4 per book. **$12 minimum.** _____

TOTAL U.S. FUNDS _____

Mail your check or money order or fill in your credit card information below:

◯ VISA   ◯ Discover   ◯ Master Card

Account Number _____

Expiration date: Month _____ Year _____

Signature **X** _____

We ship UPS to the 48 states, so please no P.O. Box addresses. PLEASE PRINT

Name _____

Street _____

City _____ State ____ Zip _____

Phone (_____) _____

Email _____

SHIPPING INFORMATION
CONTINENTAL U.S.: We ship via UPS ground service. Most customers will receive their orders within 10 business days.

ALASKA, HAWAII, U.S. MILITARY ADDRESSES AND US TERRITORIES: We ship via U.S. Priority Mail. Orders generally arrive within 2 weeks.

OUTSIDE U.S.: We generally ship via Air Mail. Delivery times vary.

RETURNS
Our books are guaranteed to please you. If they do not, return them within 30 days and we'll refund the full purchase price.

PRIVACY
We respect your privacy. We will not sell, rent or trade your personal information.

INQUIRIES AND ORDERS
Phone: (800) 688-5375
Fax: (888) 663-7855 TOLL FREE
Write: *Writing Strands*
                624 W. University, Suite 248T
                Denton, TX 76201-1889
E-mail: info@writingstrands.com
Website: www.writingstrands.com

Writing Strands

TO ORDER EVEN FASTER, GO ONLINE AT:
www.writingstrands.com